PRICE PRITCHETT

OUTSOURCED

The Employee Handbook

12 New Rules for Running Your Career in an Interconnected World

Careers just aren't

what they used to be,

are they?

You join some outfit, and the next thing you know the part you work for gets pulled out and plugged into a completely different company. You get no say in the deal.

Makes it tough to plan your job future because organizations won't sit still. They're constantly reshaping themselves. Today's business landscape keeps shifting as companies merge, restructure, reengineer, downsize and—now the latest trend—*outsource*.

As usual, people get caught in the middle.

Of course, sometimes it works out great. On other occasions it causes a career relapse. Almost always it's a gut-wrenching experience that puts you on the edge of your seat until you figure out just how you'll be affected.

We might as well get used to all this. What you're witnessing here is a revolution. A worldwide upheaval is underway as we enter the Information Age. The old organization model is coming apart. And so is our familiar concept of careers.

It may not make you feel any better about the situation, but being outsourced means you're in the mainstream. You're where the action is. You're getting the hang of what it's going to be like in the years to come.

So go to school on this. The people who get with the program are the ones who'll come out ahead. The folks who figure out how to win in the new scheme of things will have an edge over everybody else.

The secret is *adaptability*. Using your energies to adjust—to take advantage of the situation—instead of fighting the inevitable.

Getting outsourced could look like a curse, but it might be a blessing. And how well you manage yourself through all this may make the difference. Almost always our destiny is determined not by what happens to us, but by how we handle what happens.

So take charge of yourself. *Now*. And build your career according to the new rules.

©Copyright Price Pritchett

This book is copyrighted material. All rights are reserved.

It is against the law to make copies of this material without getting specific written permission in advance from Pritchett & Associates, Inc. No part of this publication may be reproduced, stored in a retrieval system, or transmitted in any form or by any means, electronic, mechanical, photocopying, recording or otherwise, without prior written permission of the publisher.

International rights and foreign translations available only through negotiation with Pritchett & Associates, Inc.

Printed in the United States of America

ISBN 0-944002-68-4

PRITCHETT & ASSOCIATES, INC.

NEW RULES

1	Shift loyalties.	page 1
2	Prepare to work in new ways.	page 5
3	Manage your "me issues."	page 9
4	Be a relationship builder.	page 13
5	Go searching for cost savings.	page 17
6	Pay attention to the new performance measures.	page 21
7	Stretch yourself.	page 25
8	Focus your energy on adapting.	page 29
9	Concentrate on the customer.	page 33
10	Protect the communication network.	page 37
11	Be a relentless learner.	page 41
12	Achieve some early wins.	page 45

NEW RULE #1: Shift loyalties.

Getting outsourced does something funny to our sense of belonging. It gives a person this vague feeling—sort of like being adopted by a stranger, and not having any say in the matter. Some people have a little trouble making the necessary emotional shift.

We might compare it to the situation where a professional athlete gets traded to another team. All of a sudden the person is wearing a different uniform, and working with a new bunch of people. The big challenge here is to put your heart into playing for the new organization.

Your natural tendency might be to mourn the passing of the old employment relationship. Nothing wrong with going through sort of a grieving process. In fact, that's just human nature.

But it's easy to romanticize the past. And to get hung up on what we don't like about the new setup. You'll see people around you focusing on the appealing parts of the old working relationship, while conveniently ignoring the more aggravating aspects of the way it's been. They'll talk longingly about "the way we were," and take a critical, gloomy view of the days to come.

If you find yourself caught in this emotional routine, challenge your thinking. A grieving process that goes on too long gets in the way of your career. It's a mindset that blinds us to opportunity and bogs us down in the past.

Now is the time to be looking forward. Thinking ahead. Searching for the promise the future holds.

To position yourself for success, you need to shift loyalties. Don't let your love for the old organization keep you from bonding with the new one. Don't let your attachment to the past prevent you from being passionate in your work today.

Transferring loyalty doesn't mean you care any less for your old company. For that matter, you may appreciate it now more than ever. But your paycheck isn't coming from the same place anymore. Another outfit provides your livelihood now.

So play like a professional—pledge allegiance to the new organization. Be willing to emotionally disconnect from your past employer, so your heart can go where your job goes.

> "You know what I hate?
>
> Indian givers...no, I take that back."
>
> *- Emo Philips*

These are the days of benchmarking…

of shooting for "best of class."

Outsourcing aligns with this strategy, but it also has a dollars and cents argument going for it. On average, companies are realizing a 9% cost savings and a 15% increase in capacity and quality through outsourcing.

The Outsourcing Institute

NEW RULE #2: Prepare to work in new ways.

Outsource firms have strong opinions about how to run their operations. And the reason they get business is because they're supposed to know how to manage it better than most people.

This means your job is bound to change.

The sort of work you do is not a sideline now. You're no longer in some secondary function, you're in the mainstream. But even if you keep doing the same thing, you can expect to do it differently. Why? Because *specialists* are fanatics about technique. They make a much bigger to-do over methodology. They operate according to carefully orchestrated moves, and you'll need to get in step as quickly as possible.

Ask yourself what's different about the outsourcer's approach. Where do you see a shift in priorities? Discover the hidden decision rules, the do's and don'ts regarding how business gets done.

While you're catching the rhythm of the work process, pay attention to the new "corporate culture." We're talking here about the personality of the place. This includes all kinds of things–from the hours people keep, to the firm's values, to the way folks communicate. Listen–learn the new employer's language–and start speaking it. Get a sense of the internal politics, how people package themselves, even the way they play. It may seem silly, but this stuff counts. It's hard to be effective if you don't fit in.

Some of the most important aspects of the culture will be subtle. Hard to read. So you need sensitive antennae, just as you need quick reflexes in the way you adjust to the new situation.

Above all, be open-minded about doing things differently. Resisting change is just wasted emotional labor. Use that energy to build your reputation as a person who gets on board.

"Sometimes it's hard to tell if something is actually a memory, or you just dreamed it. So I asked my boss if I called him a lying, stinking thief, or I just dreamed it, and he said I just dreamed it. Whew, that was close."

- *Jack Handey in* Fuzzy Memories

Outsourcing is nothing less than a full-fledged business megatrend, both here in the U.S. and around the world. And you're part of it.

Curious about just how big this trend has already become?
U.S. organizations spent $100 billion on outsourced services in 1996, with a projected growth rate of 35% into 1997.

The Outsourcing Institute

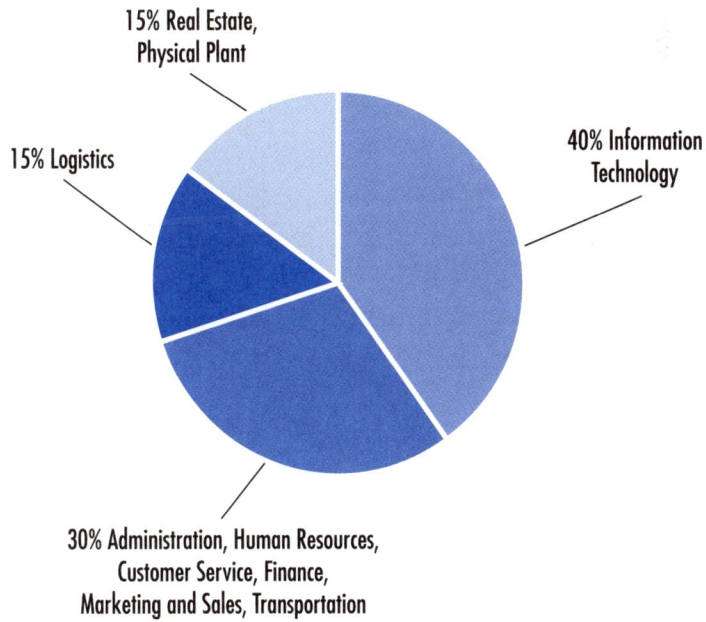

1996 U.S. Outsourcing Expenditures $100 Billion

- 15% Real Estate, Physical Plant
- 15% Logistics
- 40% Information Technology
- 30% Administration, Human Resources, Customer Service, Finance, Marketing and Sales, Transportation

The Outsourcing Institute

NEW RULE #3: Manage your "me issues."

Going through outsourcing hits some people as a jarring experience. They may see it as a threat to their livelihood. It may come as a blow to their pride or ego. Or they may simply find it frustrating having to go through the adjustment process with a new employer they didn't *personally* choose.

You see people react with a wide range of emotions. On the negative side there's uncertainty, anger or fear. And the more upset the person is, the more feelings are revealed in problem behaviors. Sometimes it shows up as resistance to change. In some cases it comes out in uncooperativeness, loss of job focus, or poor quality of work. One way or another, negative feelings usually interfere with our performance. And whether it's just moderate dissatisfaction, or despair that dominates a person's consciousness, emotions that are poorly managed put a career at risk.

Instead of falling prey to bad feelings about the situation, take charge of your temperament. Now's the time to flex your emotional muscles. To exercise self-control in the way you handle your feelings.

It's natural for your energy and attention to migrate toward the "me issues"-for example, "What's going to happen to me?" You want to know, "Will I still have a job?…Who will I report to?…Will my duties change?…How will my pay and benefits be affected?" And so on. Nobody likes waiting on those answers, and you may be dissatisfied with some of them when they finally arrive.

But this is a time for patience. Give yourself enough space to gain perspective. Stay cool. Channel your emotional energies into productive work. Depersonalize the situation. One measure of our maturity is objectivity, the ability to look at things without letting feelings color our thinking. And a good gauge of our mental health is the capacity to come to grips with things we can't change.

You gain strength if you approach the situation with positive expectancy. So entertain a spirit of hopefulness. Replace any resentment with raw curiosity. You're much more likely to find the good in this if you go looking for it, if you actively search for the positive aspects. Even if the situation looks bleak on the surface, consider how you can turn it to your advantage. Keep in mind the words of Napoleon Hill, who said, "Every adversity carries with it the seed of an equivalent or greater benefit."

> "I lost my parents at the beach when
>
> I was a kid. I asked a lifeguard
>
> to help me find them.
>
> He said, 'I don't know, kid, there are
>
> so many places they could hide.'"
>
> *- Rodney Dangerfield*

Not long ago, companies considered anything that touched the customer too business-critical for outsourcing.

The data suggests that businesses are now recognizing that most functional areas are too business-critical *not* to consider outsourcing! For example, finance, information technology, and marketing and sales now represent half of all outsourcing activity.

The Outsourcing Institute

NEW RULE #4: Be a relationship builder.

Part of your job is to help build and protect the outsourcing relationship with the client. This means you must pay attention to the people side of the deal.

These are the days of "relationship-based competition," where the quality of relations with the client is what positions the outsourcer to keep the business. This means you need to go beyond just having the technical skills needed to do your work. You need to *connect* with the customer. It's important to be compatible...easy to work with...totally reliable. Your behavior should foster trust, and serve as a bridge between the two organizations.

Another one of your personal job responsibilities is to bond with the client. To help create interpersonal ties that bind. The idea is to engineer a sense of partnership, because that often spells the difference between success or failure of the outsourcing contract.

Spend time getting to know your customer. Take pains to build relations with the people there, and be serious about understanding their business. Go out of your way to create good communication linkages. Also, do your part to prevent conflict. Be the sort of person who's known for smoothing over problems, instead of causing them.

If members of the client organization genuinely enjoy working with you, they try a lot harder to help you untangle whatever technical problems you run into. They become allies instead of adversaries. They're also far more forgiving of mistakes if they trust you and like you as a human being.

Cultivating relationships makes your job easier, even as it builds your firm's reputation. It also adds to your value as an employee, and that gives you more job security.

So do what it takes to work closely and wear well with the client. Make sure your presence contributes to the connective tissue between the two organizations.

> "I'm very loyal in a relationship.
>
> Any relationship.
>
> When I go out with my mom,
>
> I don't look at other moms.
>
> I don't go, 'Oooh, I wonder what her
>
> macaroni and cheese tastes like.'"
>
> *- Gary Shandling*

The traditional integrated firm
is not the only, nor necessarily the best,
way to create value—especially in the
global economy of the 1990s.

Today, almost any organization can gain access to resources. What differentiates companies now is their intellectual capital, their knowledge, and their expertise – not the size and scope of the resources they own and manage.

As a result, outsourcing is being adopted by firms from across the corporate spectrum. No firm is too large or too small to consider outsourcing.

The Outsourcing Institute

NEW RULE #5: Go searching for cost savings.

Outsourcing contracts are designed with a financial angle in mind. Both parties to the deal believe the arrangement is in their financial best interests.

For example, the outsource firm counts on using economies of scale to bring costs down. Or believes that it can save money because it has better technology and a keener understanding of how to run the business. Likewise, the client counts on coming out ahead in one way or another.

But to increase the odds that it really will pan out well for both sides, people at all levels need to pay attention and look for opportunities to economize. Everybody should be thinking about cost control. You, along with all the rest, must try to save money.

Most employees haven't been trained to protect the bottom line this way. They basically think in terms of just "doing the job." And that notion doesn't include the idea of any personal responsibility for the organization's overall economic health.

Take profit margins, for example. People generally look at that as management's responsibility. But if you make a habit of figuring out how to do things more efficiently, *you* help the profit picture.

In today's marketplace—where inflation is low, and competition is tough—it's hard to raise prices. So to make more money, companies need to perform functions less expensively. This calls for more cost-consciousness on the part of all employees.

When you find ways to cut costs and save money, you personally can increase the value of the outsourcing agreement. And naturally, that makes you a more valuable person to have around.

Show that you have good commercial instincts—stay on the lookout for cost savings.

> "You know why dogs have no money?
> No pockets. 'Cause they see change
> on the street all the time
> and it's driving them crazy.
> When you're walking him,
> he is always looking up at you,
> 'There's a quarter...'"
>
> *- Jerry Seinfeld*

Prestigious Fortune 500 organizations are adopting outsourcing as a cornerstone of their efforts to sharpen market focus, capitalize on global opportunities and re-energize operations.

At the same time, smaller, rapidly expanding companies are using outsourcing as a way to deliver all the capabilities of a large firm without the expense and delay of directly acquiring and managing each new resource needed.

A good example is Topsy Tail Company, with sales of over $80 million and only three employees. The "company" is actually a carefully structured network of 20 outside relationships with vendors who handle everything, from making the company's signature hair care product to the servicing of retail accounts.

The Outsourcing Institute

NEW RULE #6:
Pay attention to the new performance measures.

Outsource firms keep score differently from most organizations. They have a contract to live up to, and that keeps them focused on a set of key performance factors.

You need to pay close attention to what your employer has committed to in its agreement with the client. Why worry about that? Because those are the measures you'll get graded on as well.

The whole idea of outsourcing rests on the promise of specialization. Because your new employer focuses on a particular service area, performance gains can be achieved. But for that to actually happen, everybody has to be aligned with the client's objectives. You need to operate with a clear sense of the performance metrics by which the outsourcer will be judged.

Make it a point to find out what results your company has contracted to deliver. Usually the client's primary objectives have to do with improvements in one or more of the following areas: quality, cost, time, volume or quantity, customer satisfaction or service level, and error rate/defects/complaints.

Your job—plain and simple—is to help the outsourcing effort meet client expectations. So what's the best way to gauge your contribution? Make sure your personal output helps the company hit its performance measures. That proves you're adding value…and that you make a meaningful difference. If your presence *doesn't* have a measurable positive effect on the key performance factors, it's hard to justify your salary.

The outsourcer's performance appraisal process may not formally evaluate you in this fashion, even though it should. Just the same, you need to know that this is how you put points on the board.

> "It just as easily could have gone the other way."
>
> *- Chicago Cubs manager Don Zimmer on his team's 4-4 record on a road trip.*

The dollar value of new outsourcing projects under consideration is nearly twice as great (175%) as the value of contracts presently in force.

Despite enormous attention already paid to outsourcing as a management tool, we are still at the beginning stages of this business revolution.

The Outsourcing Institute

NEW RULE #7: Stretch yourself.

Specialist firms set high standards for performance. Their reputation in the marketplace demands an image of expertise, and that calls for excellence on the part of individual employees.

Keep in mind that companies turn to outsourcing so they can gain access to the best practices. Because they hope to benefit from using an outfit that has the luxury of focusing on one particular service or function. They're looking for superior methods. State of the art technology and processes. Clients expect the outsource firm to demonstrate a high commitment to quality—in its people, as well as in its approach.

This confronts you with a new level of accountability in the way you carry out your job responsibilities.

You can't satisfy these clients with second rate services. Offer up mediocre talent, and you're in trouble.

This is an unusually competitive playing field, but the good news is it can bring out your best. High expectations keep us on our toes. Another thing that makes us stretch is being challenged by our own coworkers. In an outsource firm, the whole company is populated with specialists, people who are experts at their crafts. This creates a rich learning environment, just as it challenges us to upgrade our skills.

Rise to the occasion. Discipline yourself to perform at high standards.

"I don't kill flies,

but I like to mess with their minds.

I hold them above globes.

They freak out and yell,

'Whooa, I'm way too high!'"

– *Bruce Baum*

You name it, somebody's ready to serve as the outsourcer. Essentially, any function in the entire organization can now be farmed out to somebody else who specializes in that particular area.

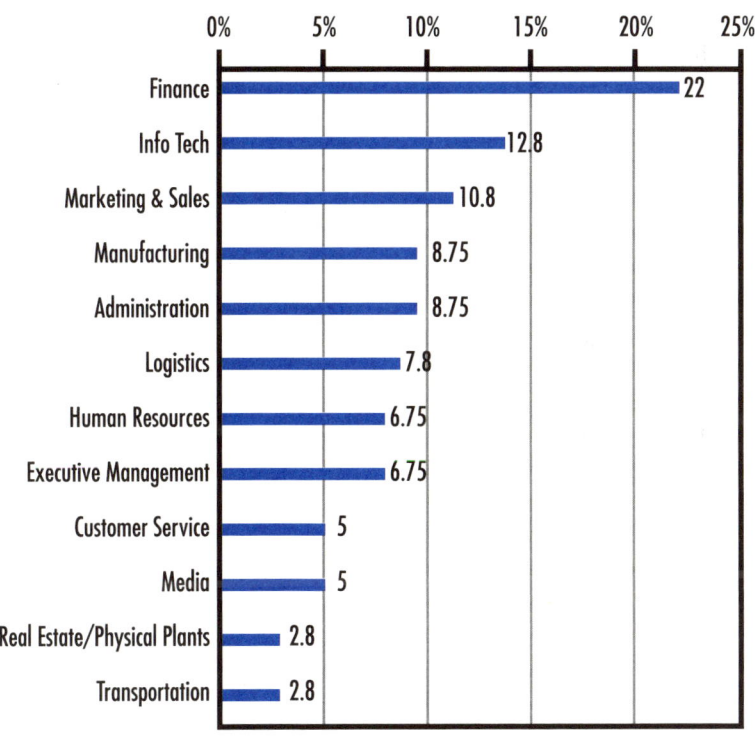

NEW RULE #8: Focus your energy on adapting.

Getting outsourced can leave people shaken. Upset with what's happened. Worried about their future. And some employees can't seem to get past these feelings.

The emotional fallout from this event is understandable. Very predictable. But that doesn't make a bad mood any less damaging to a person's career. It's not the kind of attitude a company can afford to indulge for long. An inability to "get over it" hurts performance. Plus, it makes a disturbing statement about a person's ability to cope and contribute in today's world of constant change.

Once the outsourcing contract is signed, it makes sense to accept it as a done deal. No good will come from grumbling about it after the fact. Nothing can be gained from carrying a grudge.

Just the same, there are those employees who take attitudinal revenge. Unwilling to buy in—to get on board—they wear their bad morale like a badge of resentment, as if to "get even" somehow.

And how do they retaliate? By resisting change. It's a no-win proposition, but it happens all the time. These people can't seem to quit fighting a war that's already over. They waste precious energy behaving in ways guaranteed to cause themselves unnecessary job stress.

All that effort, and what's the payoff? Nothing but problems.

There's a much better argument for adopting a go-forward attitude. For putting the past behind you, where it belongs, and focusing your emotional energy on making the most of the new situation. While a lot of important issues lie beyond your control, nobody else is in as good a position as you are to manage your morale.

You may feel like a victim of circumstance, but you're free to choose how you'll react. Choose the attitude and actions that make you most valuable as an employee.

> "If life was fair, Elvis would be alive and all the impersonators would be dead."
>
> *- Johnny Carson*

Outsourcing reaches well beyond the boundaries of the business world. Federal, state and local governments are climbing on the bandwagon in an effort to reduce costs while improving public services.

It no longer matters whether you work in the public or private sector, in a profit or not-for-profit organization, you'll be watching a growing shift toward outsourcing.

The Outsourcing Institute

NEW RULE #9: Concentrate on the customer.

Working for an outsource firm is a different ballgame. Instead of being embedded deep inside some organization, you're selling your services. There's a good old-fashioned customer out there buying what *you* have to offer.

Of course, in the strict sense of the word, there's always been a customer somewhere off in the distance. But you're no longer insulated from client issues. You're operating at close range now, probably dealing with their demands personally. This presents the need for a reassessment of your priorities.

Those darn customers always seem to require attention. It's hard to keep them satisfied. And they definitely bring some new dimensions to your job.

"Paying customers" get pushy. They expect a high level of responsiveness on your part. Considering the price tag you carry, they count on getting outstanding customer service. The way they look at it, keeping them happy is the essence of your job.

To pull that off, you need a clear understanding of the client's goals. More specifically, what is the client trying to accomplish...what is the rationale for outsourcing? Knowing this is fundamental to your success as a service provider. If you have a handle on the customer's underlying expectations, and you align with those objectives, you get the best mileage out of your efforts. Without the guidance of good insight into the client, you might try twice as hard and still fail.

Basically, you're supposed to help the client achieve its strategic business objectives. That sounds complicated. But what it boils down to is ordinary stuff. Like saving money. Taking advantage of expertise. Improving quality. Tightening turnaround time. Serving someone better than before. And so on.

Just make sure you know what your client is shooting for. Then focus on making that happen.

> "Some women hold up dresses that are so ugly and they always say the same thing. 'This looks much better on.' On what? On fire?"
>
> - Rita Rudner

In companies with over $80 million in sales, approximately 15% of functional areas are currently involved in some outsourcing activity.

We'll be seeing more and more "virtual corporations" where almost every functional area is outsourced.

Relative Use of Outsourcing Within Major Functional Areas

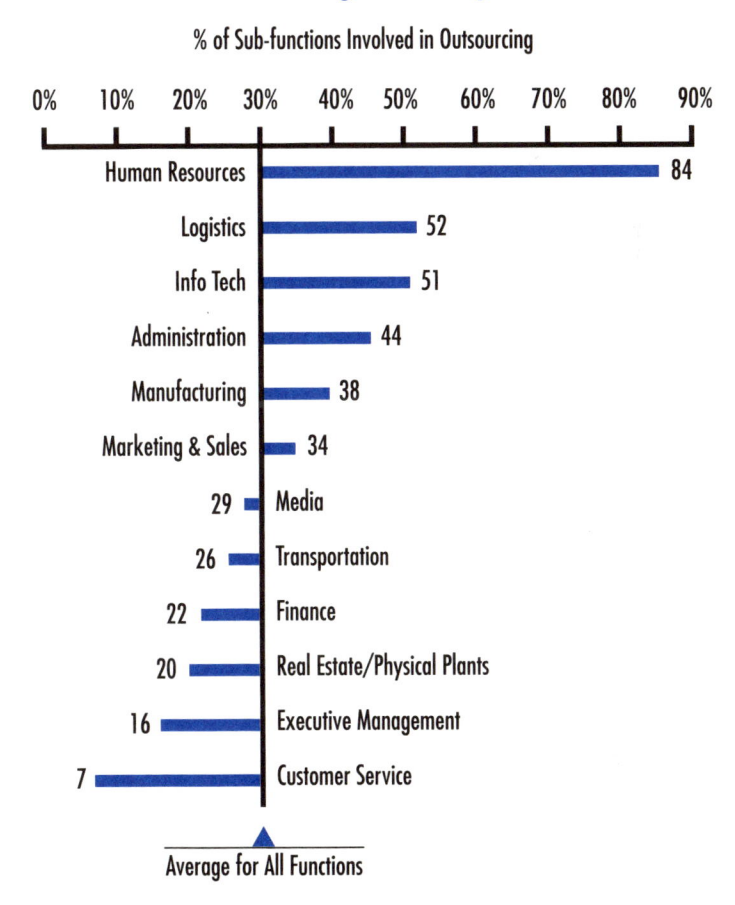

% of Sub-functions Involved in Outsourcing

Functional Area	%
Human Resources	84
Logistics	52
Info Tech	51
Administration	44
Manufacturing	38
Marketing & Sales	34
Media	29
Transportation	26
Finance	22
Real Estate/Physical Plants	20
Executive Management	16
Customer Service	7

Average for All Functions

The Outsourcing Institute and Dun & Bradstreet

NEW RULE #10:
Protect the communication network.

Outsourcing raises the curiosity level across an organization. In particular, the people who are being repositioned in their employment crave more information than usual. Problem is, their own behavior often complicates the communication process.

Look around. You can see this happening from where you sit.

People get caught up in gossip. By feeding the rumor mill, they add to the confusion. By overfocusing on problems, they lose sight of opportunities. In listening so hard for sounds of trouble, they can't seem to hear the high notes that carry good news. Because they let emotions distort the airwaves, they cause information warp that works to everyone's disadvantage.

Some of the communication problems lie beyond your reach. You don't cause them, and you're not in a position to cure them. You just have to put up with those headaches. But there are other problems you can help address.

Let's start with the basics, the fundamental "blocking and tackling" of good communication. To begin with, in dealing with outsourcing issues, you need to practice unemotional listening. Keep your feelings out of your first interpretations. Pay hard attention to messages, taking in the words without personalizing what you hear. Let your head sort through the information objectively before your heart gets involved.

Ask for clarification instead of jumping to conclusions. Seek out answers instead of speculating or going on guesswork. Got a problem? Step forward—explain what you need and why you need it. Offer solid reasons to support your request. If you have concerns, share them without getting emotional. Avoid approaching others in a way that would put them on the defensive.

You also need to run your own reality check on the rumor mill. If you "heard it through the grapevine," there's a good chance you should validate it before you believe it or pass it along.

Good communication is precious, but it doesn't come easy during change. Do your part to help the flow of accurate information.

> "My girlfriend says I never listen to her.
> I think that's what she said."
>
> *- Drake Sather*

More and more, market leaders in all industry sectors are turning to outsourcing as a way to build and sustain competitive advantage.

It works for Nike, for the city of Houston, and for the federal Department of Defense, producing impressive results in terms of competitive advantage, cost structures and market value.

Perhaps most importantly, outsourcing is a megatrend that can play to your career advantage.

The Outsourcing Institute

NEW RULE #11: Be a relentless learner.

The outsource firm employs you in order to add to its bank of know-how. The client uses you in hopes of obtaining "best in class" technical skills. Both are looking for people with real expertise. And both count on you keeping yourself highly proficient in your work.

This calls for an on-going personal commitment to self-development. Of course, there's a good chance your employer will invest in your training too. And you may well end up with better chances than you had in the past for career advancement. But you're the person with final responsibility for making yourself competent and promotable.

It used to be that the most important thing was "what you know." Today, it's how quickly you can learn something new.

Mastery of your craft requires constant effort because things change so fast these days. According to the National Research Council, it now takes only three to five years for fifty percent of a person's skills to become outdated. So we can't be content with the idea of simply *getting* an education—we have to focus on *keeping* it.

You should create a variety of learning opportunities for yourself, while also taking advantage of those provided by your employer. Get training on how to use the latest tools and methods. Study up on the hottest trends in your field. Put in the practice needed to give yourself good command of your job.

Chances are you'll need to spend some of your personal time on keeping your skills up to date. On building your repertoire. You'll be too busy during work hours to devote adequate time to development. Just remember—your competencies are the true source of job security, not who you work for.

Pursuing know-how protects your career. It's a big part of building your future.

> "My grandfather invented Cliff's Notes.
>
> It all started back in 1912...
>
> well, to make a long story short..."
>
> *- Steven Wright*

The trend lines show rapidly increasing traffic in outsourcing. Some people predict a $200 billion market by the year 2000.

The Outsourcing Index

Index of Future Outsourcing Activity. Second Quarter 1996 = $100 Billion

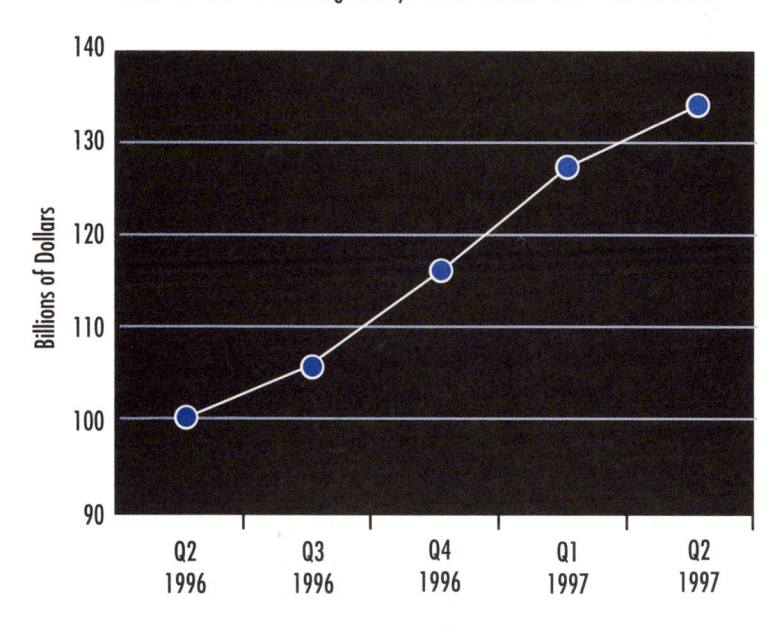

Quarter	Billions of Dollars
Q2 1996	100
Q3 1996	106
Q4 1996	116
Q1 1997	127
Q2 1997	134

The Outsourcing Institute and Dun & Bradstreet

NEW RULE #12: Achieve some early wins.

As the cowboys would say, you're riding for a new outfit now. And in some ways, you have to earn your spurs all over again.

You've got credentials, of course, including your track record. But that counts only to the extent that it gets you the job. The challenge now is to prove yourself. To satisfy this new employer that you can contribute well beyond what you add to payroll costs.

You might be upset with the thought of having to go through this drill again, especially if you were well established in your last work role. In fact, some people will presume it's the outsource firm's responsibility to make them feel wanted. They sit back and wait for the new company to show itself worthy of their talents.

Well, that's one way to approach the situation. But it's not the most astute or promising strategy. A better game plan is to go out of your way to be a playmaker.

You should know that the new employer will be sizing you up. Seeing how you fit in. Silently wondering, "What have you done for me lately?" The smart money would tell you to start building your reputation from day one. Instead of letting the usual grace period slip away without you impressing anybody, come off the line fast.

Do a quick reconnaissance. Size up the situation, and pick a couple of targets that let you play to your strengths. Apply yourself—*immediately*—and produce a rapid set of results. Early wins give you a foothold. They catch attention, command respect, and reestablish you in the new scheme of things.

A fair number of people will be focusing on the negatives. They'll be preoccupied with the problems that, frankly, just come natural to organizational change. Don't join this crowd of complainers. Instead, associate with the doers, the movers and shakers who are already making good things happen.

Seize the moment. Show that you can score.

> "My mother said, 'You won't amount to anything because you procrastinate.' I said, 'Just wait.'"
>
> *- Judy Tenuta*

Quick-Impact Training

This four-hour workshop specifically addresses what people must do to transition quickly and smoothly to a new employer when their job is outsourced to an external provider. It teaches employees to take ownership of their career by providing the tools and advice they need to maintain their competence, increase their change-adaptability and connect with new organizational and customer cultures quickly.

Based on this handbook, the workshop explains:

- The business case for outsourcing, including an explanation of how outsourcing is helping organizations gain competitive advantage

- How outsourcing disturbs organizational fit and action-oriented advice for how employees can reconnect quickly

- Three core competencies employees must acquire to run their careers effectively in an interconnected world

- Three predictable shockwaves that shatter organizational effectiveness during outsourcing

- Six "change pains" that can cause a serious drop in productivity and morale if left unmanaged

- Action guidelines to help employees recognize and capitalize on the opportunities outsourcing brings

For more information about this training program, call 1-800-992-5922.

Management Consulting Services

Pritchett & Associates' management consultants help clients successfully plan and implement large-scale strategic change. We've been improving the competitiveness of both large and small companies for over two decades—combining our knowledge and experience with an analytic, results-oriented project management approach.

Our consulting group will help you:

- Develop a strategically managed process to protect productivity during an outsourcing transition

- Capitalize on new synergies during difficult merger and joint venture integrations

- Face the organizational challenges associated with the implementation of new information technology

- Redirect your culture to foresee and maximize strategic possibilities

- Create the architecture for continued success and competitive advantage

---

If you would like to talk to one of our consultants about your unique organizational challenges, please call us at 1-888-852-1250

Books By Price Pritchett

* *Outsourced: The Employee Handbook: 12 New Rules for Running Your Career in an Interconnected World*

  Mindshift: The Employee Handbook for Understanding the Changing World of Work

* *New Work Habits for a Radically Changing World*

* *Firing Up Commitment During Organizational Change*

  Resistance: Moving Beyond the Barriers to Change

* *Business As UnUsual: The Handbook for Managing and Supervising Organizational Change* (Co-authored with Ron Pound)

* *The Employee Handbook for Organizational Change* (Co-authored with Ron Pound)

* *Team ReConstruction: Building a High Performance Work Group During Change* (Co-authored with Ron Pound)

* *Teamwork: The Team Member Handbook*

* *High-Velocity Culture Change: A Handbook for Managers* (Co-authored with Ron Pound)

* *Culture Shift: The Employee Handbook for Changing Corporate Culture*

  The Ethics of Excellence

* *A Survival Guide to the Stress of Organizational Change* (Co-authored with Ron Pound)

* *Service Excellence!*

  Smart Moves: A Crash Course on Merger Integration Management (Co-authored with Ron Pound)

* *Mergers: Growth in the Fast Lane* (Co-authored with Robert D. Gilbreath)

  The Employee Survival Guide to Mergers and Acquisitions

  After the Merger: The Authoritative Guide for Integration Success

  Making Mergers Work: A Guide to Managing Mergers and Acquisitions

  The Quantum Leap Strategy

  you^2: A High-Velocity Formula for Multiplying Your Personal Effectiveness in Quantum Leaps

---

* *Training program also available. Please call 1-800-622-8989 for more information. Call 972-789-7999 for information regarding international rights and foreign translations.*

ORDER FORM

OUTSOURCED

The Employee Handbook

12 New Rules for Running Your Career in an Interconnected World

1-99 copies	____ copies at $6.95 each
100-999 copies	____ copies at $6.75 each
1,000-4,999 copies	____ copies at $6.50 each
5,000-9,999 copies	____ copies at $6.25 each
10,000 or more copies	____ copies at $6.00 each

Name _____

Job Title _____

Organization _____

Phone _____

Street Address _____ Zip _____

P.O. Box _____ Zip _____

City, State _____

Country _____

Purchase order number (if applicable) _____

Applicable sales tax, shipping and handling charges will be added. Prices subject to change.

Orders less than $100 require prepayment. $100 or more may be invoiced.

☐ Check Enclosed   ☐ Please Invoice

☐ VISA   ☐ MasterCard   ☐ American Express

Account Number _____ Expiration Date _____

Signature _____

08705 335555

Pritchett & Associates Inc.
P O Box 19750 London SW15 5ZT
Tel 08705 335555   Fax 08705 168134

KA7494

Price Pritchett is Chairman and CEO of Pritchett & Associates, Inc., a Dallas-based firm specializing in mergers, outsourcing and organizational change. He has authored over 20 books on individual and organizational performance, and is recognized internationally as a leading authority on the dynamics of change. He holds a Ph.D. in psychology and has consulted to top executives in major corporations for over two decades.